Seasons of the Marsh

Janet Powers

Happy birthday Harry!
All the best Joni!

Janet

© copyright 2005

ISBN 0-9770624-1-4

Janet Powers
The Gallery on Newcastle
1626 Newcastle Street
Brunswick, GA 31520

www.thegalleryonnewcastle.com • www.janetpowers-artist.com

Book Design by Joe Loehle, Crawdad Studio & Gallery, Inc., St. Simons Island, GA

Photography by Harlan Hambright, Crawdad Studio & Gallery, Inc., St. Simons Island, GA

Editing by Lucy Loehle, St. Simons Island, GA

Printed in Hong Kong

TABLE OF CONTENTS

IN MEMORY

In memory of my grandmother, Rosalie Mitchener Covington, and my dad, Thomas Thomas Covington, who both passed on to me an innate and devout reverence for Nature.

ACKNOWLEDGEMENTS

I wish to acknowledge my mother Genevieve Mestayer Covington, who loves to say "she got her talent from me... and she got it all." I so value her unending love, encouragement, pride, and generosity.

My former husband, and current friend, Alex Powers taught me most of what I know about painting—not only the fundamentals, but also the passion of making art.

Mack Sullivan, for his faithful support of local art.

And finally my dear husband Paul Stanton who has given unending encouragement and faithful support, allowing me the ability to live my passion. I don't know from where he got his patience, but he, too, must have gotten it all!

FOREWORD

Janet Powers is a truly visionary artist who enjoys painting romantic vistas of the watery estuaries and the Marshes of Glynn. She has developed her own enchanting style which captures the mood and atmospheric qualities of the dramatic marshes that surround her studio. Although Janet's current work is in constant demand, she keeps her eye toward the future as she continues to modify her style. Constantly changing her palette, she simplifies her subject matter to create yet another dramatic abstracted canvas. Some features in her recent work include romantic clouds, grayed blue skies and green watery marshes. Her paintings bring drama and life to any private or corporate collection. Each painting adds a distinct note of beauty and form to any home or office.

On a personal note, it has been a privilege to collaborate with Janet on many projects. Her professional manner and quiet enthusiasm make her a pleasure to work with. This joie de vivre of creativity produces many inspiring mural-like paintings for clients ranging from major corporations to private individuals.

Something new is always on the horizon for Janet Powers, artist *extraordinaire*. I look forward to continuing to work with this ever-growing and ever-changing artist who has made Coastal Georgia her home.

~Mildred Huie "Millie" Wilcox
President, Left Bank Art Gallery
St. Simons Island, Georgia

ARTIST'S STATEMENT

This southern coast of Georgia is one of the "special" places I've seen. Paul and I would drive through the area on the way to visit our daughter who was attending Florida State University in Tallahassee, and we would feel a fierce attraction. Even though I'd painted very few landscapes in my almost 30-year art career, I felt compelled to come back here to paint this landscape. The most interesting thing is that I've painted these salt marshes almost exclusively since we moved here eight years ago. People frequently ask if it's not tiring to paint the same subject matter for so long. While I've always felt it important to work in a series, I frequently changed subject matter to avoid boredom; well, never has a series held my attention for such a long period of time as these marshes. How could one possibly become tired of looking at or painting a subject with incessant changes? This land simply has its own vitality and spirit.

As artists, we tend to paint our surroundings, and I feel so fortunate to be allowed to be a part of the environment that evokes such passion in me.

Plein Air versus Studio Painting

I find increasing value in painting on location, mainly because it affords the opportunity to experience the essence of nature's gifts. Painting and drawing both induce another whole dimension of "seeing," and being "there" allows the painter to see and feel what cannot be seen or felt from a photograph. To watch the cast shadow of a cloud move steadily across a large expanse of marsh is amazing.

On the other hand, when one is "there," one tends to see too much. There is so much detail in the vision that it's very difficult, without a great deal of experience, to eliminate the extraneous matter and focus on the design of the rectangle. There are too many real but small shapes – leaves, branches, blades of grass – that are unimportant to the painting. I figured early on that I'd rather be a poet than a narrator and, therefore, simplicity has become very important to my work. That means fewer shapes and more color harmony. For this reason only, painting from a photograph has its own value. It helps to simplify.

So, then, it seems a balance of the two is just fine. There are times when painting without a photograph is impractical, if not impossible, because of the conditions or the subject—inclement weather, a moving target, a difficult pose. So, while I paint on location at every opportunity (and have had to dig gnats out of the oils with my palette knife on more than one occasion), I don't do penance if I find myself in the cozy comfort of my studio.

William Pachner tells about four men in a hospital room, only one of whom had a view out the window. It was he, of course, who described the beautiful scenery and lush vistas for the others, who all became jealous and decided to murder him so that they could take turns at the window. After they murdered him, they discovered that the window looked out onto a brick wall, and they realized that they had murdered the one man among them who could create great beauty from within himself for others to enjoy. This is what the artist does.

Shades of Night

34x42 OIL ON CANVAS

SPRING

Spring is my favorite time of year by far. Along with all of nature, I begin to warm up and stir from the long winter's nap. The birds are so excited—some become raucous in their enthusiasm and others are melodious with their song. Vegetation takes on glows of various yellow-greens to reds from the newly formed buds. The variety of greens is visually striking. The cedars retain their deep, rich darkness, contrasting with a range of colors and values.

It's the time of year when it's wonderful and *comfortable* to be outside. With the visual stimuli, nothing is as satisfying as being there in person to capture the awakening on a canvas!

"These salt marshes are very animated and alive, teeming with wildlife and waterfowl. The constant changes are due to the ever-changing light, the ebb and flow of the tides, the atmospheric conditions, and the seasons. The colors of the grasses range from myriads of greens in the spring and summer, to mauves, browns and burgundy in the winter."

~ Janet Powers

HOG ISLAND

16X20 OIL ON CANVAS

Marsh from Kiawah Bridge

18X24 OIL ON CANVAS

"Rather than just documenting the landscapes as they are, my paintings are meant to portray a mood. There-fore, I use a somewhat monochromatic color scheme and at times purposely keep the values close in range so as not to detract from the mood."

~ Janet Powers

Windswept Grass

11X14 OIL ON CANVAS

DARKER SHADE OF EVENING

8X10 OIL ON CANVAS

THE QUIET OF STILL

16X20 OIL ON CANVAS

CEDAR REFLECTIONS

11X14 OIL ON PANEL

FOREGROUND YUCCA

9X12 OIL ON CANVAS

WINDOW OF OPPORTUNITY

18X24 OIL ON CANVAS

PRIVATE COLLECTION, PONTE VEDRA, FLORIDA

DISTANT SUNSET

11X14 OIL ON PANEL

MOOD OF DAY'S END

8X10 OIL ON CANVAS

"Paul is always afraid I'm going to be struck by lightning. In the spring and summer we get violent storms moving in rapidly, and I rush out to the dock to try to capture some of that excitement and energy with oil paints or charcoal."

~ Janet Powers

APPROACHING RAIN

11X14 OIL ON CANVAS

EVENING GLOW

24x30 OIL ON CANVAS

PRIVATE COLLECTION, ST. SIMONS ISLAND, GEORGIA

THERE'S A HUSH

16X20 OIL ON CANVAS

"Artists don't get down to work until the pain of working is exceeded by the pain of not working."

~Stephan DeSaebler

THE EVERETTS' TIDAL CREEK

12x16 OIL ON CANVAS

PRIVATE COLLECTION, SEA ISLAND, GEORGIA

Big River

24x18 OIL ON CANVAS

Private Collection, Sea Island, Georgia

"The heat lightning moving horizontally across the sky is my favorite! It's like two gods are up there, tossing the lightning bolt back and forth to each other. It can last for eons!"

~ Janet Powers

FROM BIRCH'S DOCK

8X10 OIL ON CANVAS

PRIVATE COLLECTION, ST. SIMONS ISLAND, GEORGIA

*"Minutes before the sun sets, and for a short while after, the marsh grass takes on shades of glorious warm glows. I think it's the reason for the name **The Golden Isles**."*

~ Janet Powers

GLIMMERING MARSH

24X30 OIL ON CANVAS

PRIVATE COLLECTION, ST. SIMONS ISLAND. GEORGIA

THE EVERETTS' WEST VIEW

24x30 OIL ON CANVAS

PRIVATE COLLECTION, SEA ISLAND. GEORGIA

Summer

Summer has a tough time following spring. The grasses in the marsh take on a green hue, and there's so much green in nature that it can become monotonous, with so much of that difficult color on one canvas. But there are redeeming qualities, such as the numerous storms and lightning shows from the heat. The long days are nice, but then I don't get to see many sunrises in the summer…

I suppose the best aspect of summer is that the "no-see-ums" prefer a little less heat. My body has gladly adapted to the heat and enjoys some gnat-free time. Painting on location is fine as long as there's a huge oak tree to provide shade with its spreading canopy.

RIFLE CUT, ALTAMAHA RIVER

18X24 OIL ON CANVAS

PRIVATE COLLECTION, SEA ISLAND, GEORGIA

MORNING MARSH

8X10 OIL ON CANVAS

"I think one's art goes as far and as deep as one's love goes. I see no reason for painting but that."

~ Andrew Wyeth

INTRACOASTAL WATERWAY FROM JEKYLL

8X10 OIL ON CANVAS

Marsh with Blue Tree Line

11X14 OIL ON CANVAS

"A fine painting is about the artist and the subject. It should be as personal as your handwriting and as intimate as your diary."

~ Glenn Bradshaw

Sunset on the Satilla

30x40 OIL ON CANVAS

PRIVATE COLLECTION, SEA ISLAND, GEORGIA

X

GLOWING HORIZON

8X10 OIL ON CANVAS

VEILED SUN

30X40 OIL ON CANVAS

CARABELLE FROM THE BRIDGE

18X24 OIL ON CANVAS

EVENING, SEA ISLAND MARSH

11X14 OIL ON CANVAS

CUMBERLAND HAMMOCK

9X12 OIL ON CANVAS

Marsh with Aqua Sky and Water

10x20 OIL ON PAPER

PRIVATE COLLECTION, SEA ISLAND, GEORGIA

REFLECTIONS

12X16 OIL ON CANVAS

PRIVATE COLLECTION. SEA ISLAND. GEORGIA

"So, what's the attraction?

Only after painting these vistas did I begin to understand the allure. There's a strong sense of vast and never-ending spaciousness. This creates mystery; one can wonder just how far "it" goes and what might be "there."

The palette is limited to soft, muted colors. There is plenty of texture, yet the shapes are simple. The distant tree lines are silhouetted forms with interesting edges accented by skies of varying moods. There is the smell of salt air, the sound of squawking seagulls, the feeling of a cool breeze mingled with the warmth of the sun or the balminess of fog, the vividly stained sky of sunset or sunrise. All combine to make the senses tingle.

This tingle is what I feel, and attempt to convey in my work."

~ Janet Powers

Salt Marsh at Dusk

11X14 OIL ON CANVAS

PRIVATE COLLECTION. OAK RIDGE, NORTH CAROLINA

Everetts' View

10x8 oil on canvas

Private Collection, Ogden, Utah

"When I eat a tomato I look at it the way anyone else would. But when I paint a tomato, then I see it differently."

~ Henri Matisse

FANCY BLUFF SUNLIT MARSH

11X14 OIL ON CANVAS

PRIVATE COLLECTION, ROSWELL, GEORGIA

"Storms are awesome: the power, the

smells, the moods! They're so humbling.

I love storms; I love to paint them!"

~ Janet Powers

OVERCAST

14X18 OIL ON CANVAS

FALL

Fall is the time for ripening. In the past it was slightly depressing to me because I had to go back to school, but since that's no longer a factor, I just enjoy it. The colors are the most vivid during this season, with the leaves becoming brilliant before dying. There are some fall grasses that turn lovely lavenders and mauves, while some greens remain. October is usually the month I give a *plein air* workshop because the temperature is perfect here in the Deep South, and sometimes the bugs aren't so bad.

"You learn how to make your work by

making your work…"

~ David Bayles and Ted Orland

Art & Fear: Observations on the

Perils (and Rewards) of Artmaking

Darien River

11X14 OIL ON CANVAS

FANCY BLUFF TREES

11X14 OIL ON CANVAS

PRIVATE COLLECTION, ST. SIMONS ISLAND, GEORGIA

CLAM CREEK IN OCTOBER

16X20 OIL ON CANVAS

PRIVATE COLLECTION, HOUSTON, TEXAS

"Some liken the experience of trying to understand unfamiliar art to that of being introduced to someone new. "It's like meeting people -- they may have a dazzling impact in the first ten minutes, but really interesting people continue to reveal themselves over the years. I look for the same thing in art."

~ Jeffrey Deitch

New York Art Dealer

SUNSET ON ANDREWS ISLAND

18X24 OIL ON CANVAS

PRIVATE COLLECTION, SEA ISLAND, GEORGIA

BLYTHE ISLAND

18x24 OIL ON CANVAS

PRIVATE COLLECTION, RED BANK, NEW YORK

Darien River in October

11x14 OIL ON CANVAS

Amelia Outfitters Marsh

16X20 OIL ON PANEL

OCTOBER CREEK AND SALT MARSH

24X30 OIL ON CANVAS

"You could not step twice in the same river; for other waters are ever flowing onto you."

~ Heraclitus

Clam Creek in the Fall

14X18 OIL ON CANVAS

Sunset on the Little Satilla

30x40 OIL ON CANVAS

PRIVATE COLLECTION, GREENVILLE, SOUTH CAROLINA

FORT KING GEORGE RIVER

14X18 OIL ON CANVAS

MOONRISE ON THE SATILLA

14X18 OIL ON CANVAS

MEANDERING SALT CREEK

9X12 OIL ON CANVAS

MARSH GRASS REFLECTED

8X10 OIL ON CANVAS

"The tidal creeks slither in and out, changing their shapes continuously. Their bodies swell and disappear like ribbons blowing in the wind."

~ Janet Powers

POSEY CREEK

12X16 OIL ON CANVAS

Janet Powers

Silent Sunset

48X60 OIL ON CANVAS

Private Collection, Darien, Connecticut

FULL MOON EVE

8X10 OIL ON CANVAS

PRIVATE COLLECTION, BRUNSWICK, GEORGIA

"Paul and I adore full moons; we have full-moon parties to celebrate them. Tonight while cooking supper we kept running out to the dock to look for it to rise. It was later than we expected, around 9:00, and we wondered if it was overcast or too cloudy to see on the horizon. But we persisted, and were rewarded.

It was so magnificent!

It was huge, peaking over the distant tree line, a bright orange glowing in the inky black sky. It was too incredible to put into words, so I committed the effects to memory, hoping to paint it. I am always curious about the reflection and how it grows longer and slowly slinks across the river until it reaches the other side. Tonight I studied it, again. Tonight I studied the glowing circle around the moon, again.

At one point, I made a 90-degree turn to see intermittent headlights on I-95, accompanied by the muted roar of tires on pavement… tires rushing to get somewhere. What a dichotomy! All of that activity compared to the stillness of that big, beautiful full moon, suspended there bigger than anything, was moving. It drew my breath; it drew my tears. How could anyone bear to not experience this wonderment?"

~ Janet Powers

FULL MOON ON THE SATILLA

24x36 OIL ON LINEN

WINTER

Winter can be anything—there can be beautiful days or brutally cold days. Two years ago I thought I'd take a chance and have the workshop in January (figuring the bugs would be asleep for sure). Well, it turned out to be a bitter cold time. We were trying to brave the icy wind, but ended up coming into the gallery at lunchtime to finish the day. Paul very smugly told us we definitely were not Lewis and Clark candidates.

The neat aspects of winter to me are the light and the variety of tree branches. The sun is low and, therefore, casts very long, deep shadows. The leafless trees present a chance for soft, blurry edges. Another bonus is that it's easy to experience sunrise without giving up too much sleep. And, best of all, spring is just around the corner.

"At one time I thought that art was something of beauty. Over the years I've learned that it's really something that creates emotion, something you haven't seen before or thought about before."

~ Eli Broad

Art Collector

VERY DISTANT TREE LINE

16X20 OIL ON CANVAS

CLAM CREEK, EARLY MORNING

8X10 OIL ON CANVAS

PRIVATE COLLECTION, SEA ISLAND, GEORGIA

VIEW FROM THE DOCK

16X20 OIL ON CANVAS

GOLDEN MARSH

12X16 OIL ON CANVAS

FROM THE BOAT RAMP

12X16 OIL ON PANEL

PRIVATE COLLECTION, PONTE VEDRA, FLORIDA

Winter Evening

12x16 OIL ON CANVAS

PRIVATE COLLECTION, CORNING, NEW YORK

Sunset, Salt Marsh

8x10 oil on canvas

Private Collection, Indianapolis, Indiana

Shades of Mauve

16x20 oil on canvas

HARVEST MOON FROM THE DOCK

8X10 OIL ON CANVAS

PRIVATE COLLECTION, ST. SIMONS ISLAND. GEORGIA

Fancy Bluff Trees, Vertical

18x14 OIL ON CANVAS

Private Collection, Houston, Texas

WINTER GRASSES

14X18 OIL ON CANVAS

PRIVATE COLLECTION, NEW BERN, NORTH CAROLINA

February Setting Sun

24x18 OIL ON CANVAS

Private Collection, Houston, Texas

Sunny Afternoon at the Griggs'

12X16 OIL ON CANVAS

"A picture is a picture of something. A painting is something."

~ Robert Henri

WINTER, CLAM CREEK

30x40 OIL ON CANVAS

PRIVATE COLLECTION, DARIEN, CONNECTICUT

ALBERT ISLAND

11X14 OIL ON CANVAS

SUN GLOW, COLONEL'S ISLAND

9X12 OIL ON CANVAS

PRIVATE COLLECTION, ST. SIMONS ISLAND, GEORGIA

Jamie Powers

"Painters must speak through paint,

not through words."

~ Hans Hoffman

THE MARSHES OF GLYNN SALUTE THE SIDNEY LANIER BRIDGE

16X20 OIL ON CANVAS

PRIVATE COLLECTION, WILMINGTON, DELAWARE

"When bankers get together for dinner, they discuss art. When artists get together for dinner they discuss money."

~ Oscar Wilde

NEARING DAY'S END

12X16 OIL ON CANVAS

THE GRIGGS' MARSH

18X24 OIL ON CANVAS

"She liked to have a show for herself before mounting a public one, as she had done in 1915 when she first decided to paint for herself. Then 'I already settled it for myself,' she candidly stated ... 'so flattery and criticism go down the same drain and I am quite free.'"

~ Laurie Lisle,

author of *Portrait of an Artist: A Biography of Georgia O'Keefe*

RUSSET MARSH

12X16 OIL ON CANVAS

PRIVATE COLLECTION, SEA ISLAND, GEORGIA

RIBAULT REFLECTIONS

11X14 OIL ON PANEL

Blythe Island River II

24x30 OIL ON CANVAS

"Buzzard Island is just down the river from us. It's unsual in this area to see a group of palms like this. I photograph it from our boat every time we ride by, and am very distressed to see the erosion. There are always palms that have fallen into the river, victims of the currents and the wakes."

~ Janet Powers

BUZZARD ISLAND

14X18 OIL ON CANVAS

Index